STUDY GUIDE

The Lord's Day

Sabbath Worship and Rest

W. Robert Godfrey

LIGONIER MINISTRIES
Renew your Mind.
LIGONIER.ORG | 800-435-4343

421 Ligonier Court, Sanford, FL 32771
Email: info@ligonier.org

Printed in China.

Contents

Introduction

Why do Christians worship on Sunday? And how is worship on the first day of the week connected to the fourth commandment? Isn't the Sabbath the seventh day of the week and not the first? These questions are important and have direct ramifications on how we worship, how we understand the Bible, and how we spend our time on what we now call the Lord's Day. In this teaching series, Dr. W. Robert Godfrey surveys the theology, history, practice, and biblical teaching behind the Lord's Day so that we might devote this day to the One to whom it rightly belongs—the Lord.

This study guide is a companion to the video teaching series. Whether you are using the DVDs, streaming the videos on Ligonier.org, or going through the course in Ligonier Connect, this resource is designed to help you make the most of the learning experience. For each message in the series, there is a corresponding lesson in this guide. Here is what you will find in each lesson:

INTRODUCTION	The introduction is a brief paragraph that summarizes the content covered in the lecture and considered in the study guide lesson. **How to use:** Use the introduction to each lesson to get a sense of the big picture before watching the video. Refer to these statements as you work through the study guide to remind yourself of what you have already covered and where you are headed.
LEARNING GOALS	The learning goals are the knowledge and skills that the study guide lesson will endeavor to equip you with as you work through the lecture content. **How to use:** Familiarize yourself with the goals of each lesson before engaging its contents. Keeping the overall purpose in mind as you watch each video and reflect on or discuss the questions will help you get the most out of each lesson.
KEY IDEAS	The key ideas are the major points or takeaways from the lecture. **How to use:** Use these ideas to prepare yourself for each lesson and to review previous lessons. They describe specifically the knowledge that each lecture is communicating.

REFLECTION & DISCUSSION QUESTIONS	The questions are the guided reflection and/or discussion component of the lesson that is intended to help you prepare for, process, and organize what you are learning. **How to use:** Reflect on individually or discuss in a group the questions in the order in which they appear in the lesson. The time stamps in the right margin indicate where the answers to questions during the video can be found.
PRAYER	The prayer section offers suggestions for how to close the lesson in prayer with respect to what was taught in the lecture. **How to use:** Consider using each lesson's prayer section as a guide to personal or group prayer. These sections follow the ACTS prayer model, which you can learn more about in R.C. Sproul's Crucial Questions booklet *Does Prayer Change Things?* This helpful guide is available as a free e-book at Ligonier.org.
REVIEW QUIZ	The review quiz is a set of six multiple-choice questions that appears at the end of each lesson. **How to use:** Use each quiz to check your comprehension and memory of the major points covered in each lecture. It will be most beneficial to your learning if you take a lesson's quiz either sometime between lessons or just before you begin the next lesson in the study guide.
ANSWER KEY	The answer key provides explanations for the reflection and discussion questions and answers to the multiple-choice questions in the review quiz. **How to use:** Use the answer key to check your own answers or when you do not know the answer. Note: Do not give in too quickly; struggling for a few moments to recall an answer reinforces it in your mind.

Study Schedules

The following table suggests four plans for working through *The Lord's Day* video teaching series and this companion study guide. Whether you are going through this series on your own or with a group, these schedules should help you plan your study path.

	Extended 8-Week Plan	**Standard 6-Week Plan**	**Abbreviated 4-Week Plan**	**Intensive 3-Week Plan**
Week	**Lesson**			
1	*	1	1	1 & 2
2	1	2	2 & 3	3 & 4
3	2	3	4 & 5	5 & 6
4	3	4	6	
5	4	5		
6	5	6		
7	6			
8	*			

* For these weeks, rather than completing lessons, spend your time discussing and praying about your learning goals for the study (the first week) and the most valuable takeaways from the study (the last week).

1

What Should We Think of Sunday?

INTRODUCTION

Throughout the history of the church, Christians have worshiped on Sunday. But the church has not always understood the significance of this day in the same way. Certainly today, many do not view it as significant at all. Things haven't always been this way. In this lesson, Dr. Godfrey surveys the recent landscape of the church concerning Sunday and begins to explain how the early church through the Middle Ages understood it in relation to the Sabbath and to the fourth commandment.

LEARNING GOALS

When you have finished this lesson, you should be able to:

- Describe recent views and practices concerning the Lord's Day
- Identify how the Lord's Day was viewed and in what manner it was connected to the fourth commandment in the early and medieval church

KEY IDEAS

- One of the greatest changes in the Christian church in the last seventy-five years has been in our attitude about Sunday.
- Cultural influences and church practice have changed the way we think about Sunday.
- The early church fathers made a sharp distinction between the Lord's Day and the fourth commandment, but the church reestablished this connection during the Middle Ages.

REFLECTION & DISCUSSION QUESTIONS

Before the Video

What Do You Think?

Take a moment to answer the following questions. They will prepare you for the lecture.

- Why are you undertaking this study about the Lord's Day?

- What do you think Sunday is all about?

Scripture Reading

Thus the heavens and the earth were finished, and all the host of them. And on the seventh day God finished his work that he had done, and he rested on the seventh day from all his work that he had done. So God blessed the seventh day and made it holy, because on it God rested from all his work that he had done in creation.

—Genesis 2:1–3

- How did God bless the seventh day and make it holy? Why is this significant?

During the Video

Answer the following questions while you watch the video. They will guide you through the lecture.

New Attitude *0:00–15:00*

- What are some indications that the church's attitude about Sunday has changed in its own practices?

- What are some reasons for this attitude change in the broader American culture?

- What are some of the negative results from this attitude change in the church?

Sunday in the Early and Medieval Church *15:00–23:51*

- Why did the early church fathers make a sharp distinction between the Lord's Day and the Jewish Sabbath?
- What important distinction allowed Thomas Aquinas to connect the Lord's Day to the fourth commandment?

After the Video

Answer the following questions after you have finished the lecture. They will help you identify and summarize the major points.

- Which do you think most influenced the other: the church's change in attitude about Sunday leading to the culture's change in attitude about Sunday or vice versa?

  If you are in a group, have the members discuss where they have seen a change in the church's or the broader culture's attitudes about Sunday.

- What is the predominant attitude about Sunday among Christians today?

  If you are in a group, have the members discuss the following question: How does either the church's practice or societal influences affect your understanding of the Lord's Day?

- Why is navigating what the early church fathers thought about Sunday difficult?

  If you are in a group, have the members discuss whether they think the Lord's Day is connected to the fourth commandment while providing some rationale for their conclusions.

PRAYER

Commit what you have learned from God's Word in this lesson to prayer.

- Praise God for His sovereign hand and work throughout history.
- Confess times when you have neglected the worship of God with His gathered people.
- Thank God for creating all things, and especially the church, for His own glory.
- Ask God to help you understand the significance of the Lord's Day.

REVIEW QUIZ

Use these multiple-choice questions to measure what you learned from this lesson.

1. Apart from the New Testament, we have testimony that Christians worshiped on the first day of the week going back to which century?
   a. Second
   b. Third
   c. Fourth
   d. Fifth

2. Why did the church fathers not connect the Lord's Day to the fourth commandment?
   a. To free Christians from the moral aspects of God's law
   b. To clarify that the church is not bound by Jewish regulations
   c. To encourage Christians' industry throughout the week
   d. To separate from early church practice

3. For a time, Jewish Christians continued to go to synagogue in the early church.
   a. True
   b. False

4. Roman Catholics combine into one which two commandments that Protestants see as separate commandments?
   a. The first and second
   b. The second and third
   c. The third and fourth
   d. The ninth and tenth

5. As little as seventy-five years ago, certain cultural practices were unthinkable on Sundays.
   a. True
   b. False

6. What two distinctions in the Mosaic law did Thomas Aquinas make to underscore the enduring significance of the fourth commandment to Christians?
   a. Moral and civil law
   b. Civil and ceremonial law
   c. Moral and ceremonial law
   d. Case and statutory law

Answer Key—What Should We Think of Sunday?

REFLECTION & DISCUSSION QUESTIONS

Before the Video

What Do You Think?

These are personal questions. The answers should be based on your own knowledge and experience.

Scripture Reading

- How did God bless the seventh day and make it holy? Why is this significant?

  God blessed the seventh day and made it holy by resting on it. He ceased creating. This provides for us God's own example of resting, a resting through which He blessed the day. His act of blessing the day and making it holy gives us another reason to observe it.

During the Video

New Attitude

- What are some indications that the church's attitude about Sunday has changed in its own practices?

  One of the greatest changes in the church in the last seventy-five years is its attitude about Sunday. Sunday is often no longer treated as a holy day. As Dr. Godfrey recounted, there was a time when a family would attend worship in the morning and spend devotional time together before returning to church to worship in the evening. Sunday evening worship is no longer practiced to the extent that it once was. In addition to this practice falling out of favor, people now spend the time that they would have spent worshiping doing other things.

- What are some reasons for this attitude change in the broader American culture?

  The changing attitude about Sunday is seen not only in the church's practice but also in the culture at large. Many reasons are hypothesized for why this has occurred. Because of the automobile, people can travel more readily. And because of television and a host of other technologies, entertainment is more widely available. Sports have become a prominent feature on any given Sunday.

- What are some of the negative results from this attitude change in the church?

  Many churches changed their approach to Lord's Day worship to adapt to the culture, thinking that they would be more evangelistically successful because of such changes. But the truth is that the church is shrinking and is no longer as influential as it once was. More than this, negative impacts are seen within the church. Christians are less knowledgeable because they are gathering for worship half as often as they would once have done.

Sunday in the Early and Medieval Church

- Why did the early church fathers make a sharp distinction between the Lord's Day and the Jewish Sabbath?

  The early church fathers made a sharp distinction between the Lord's Day and the Jewish Sabbath because they essentially wanted to see a break between Jewish and Christian practices. They did not want the life of the church to be controlled by the synagogues and, as a result of that, by Mosaic regulations.

- What important distinction allowed Thomas Aquinas to connect the Lord's Day to the fourth commandment?

  The church's thought about the connection between the Lord's Day and the fourth commandment changed over time. Thomas Aquinas saw in the fourth commandment both a ceremonial and a moral aspect. For this reason, he believed that the fourth commandment applied to Christians morally but that the seventh-day observance of the fourth commandment did not, since that was only a ceremonial aspect of the law.

After the Video

- Which do you think most influenced the other: the church's change in attitude about Sunday leading to the culture's change in attitude about Sunday or vice versa?

  This is a challenging question to reflect on, and certainly both the church and the culture influenced each other. It seems that the church may have been more influenced by the culture. Dr. Godfrey references many reasons behind this, including rapid changes in transportation and entertainment, as well as what the church perceived needed to be done to have an evangelistic influence on the culture. Whether the church or the culture most changed the way people think about Sunday, the church is facing detrimental results to its health within and to its influence without.

- What is the predominant attitude about Sunday among Christians today?

  Your answer may reflect your own circles within evangelicalism, but with most churches' meeting once for worship on the Lord's Day and the norms of our culture at large, the predominant opinion about Sunday for many Christians seems to be that, besides worship, Sunday is free for us to do with it what we want.

- Why is navigating what the early church fathers thought about Sunday difficult?

  The early church fathers didn't connect the Lord's Day to the fourth commandment, and this poses a difficulty for us because it might be assumed that the church was so closely connected to the Apostolic church that it would indicate something about the New Testament church's own thought and practice. But we must consider the historical context of the church and the difficulties that began to arise between Jews and Christians, between synagogues and churches. The church fathers' impulse to make a sharp distinction between the Lord's Day and the Sabbath, in this light, is understandable.

REVIEW QUIZ

1. **A.**
   The New Testament bears witness that Christians met on the first day of the week to worship. We also have extrabiblical testimony of this. The Epistle to Barnabas, dating back to the second century and possibly earlier, is one such example.

2. **B.**
   It may be surprising to learn that the church fathers did not connect the Lord's Day to the fourth commandment. Historical context is key for understanding why they did not. The church was in a time of transition. The church fathers did not want the church to be bound by certain Mosaic regulations, just as the Apostle Paul defended the church in his day.

3. **A.**
   Jewish Christians still attended synagogue while also worshiping on the first day in the early church. Historical testimony to this fact can be seen in such places as the Epistle to Barnabas and other rabbinic literature. Over time, tensions developed that would bring this practice to an end.

4. **A.**
   Roman Catholics divide the Ten Commandments differently from Protestants. They combine the first two commandments into one. In order to end up with Ten Commandments, Roman Catholics then split the tenth commandment in two. This is important to remember for clarity's sake when engaging with a Roman Catholic and even some Lutherans who follow this practice.

5. **A.**
   Dr. Godfrey told several stories that highlighted the influence on society at large of the church's setting apart the first day of the week as holy. Certain parts of stores were sectioned off, and even some roads were closed down in areas. People thought the National Football League wouldn't succeed because its games are played and televised on Sundays.

6. **C.**
   Reformed theologians continue to think of the Mosaic law in terms of a threefold division: moral, civil, and ceremonial. Thomas Aquinas asserted that the fourth commandment had moral and ceremonial aspects. He primarily understood the ceremonial aspects of this commandment as related to seventh-day observance.

2

Historical & Biblical Reflections

INTRODUCTION

Over the course of history, there have been different periods of thought concerning the Lord's Day. The early post-Apostolic church didn't connect the Lord's Day to the fourth commandment, but this connection was made, though not perfectly, by Thomas Aquinas. In this lesson, Dr. Godfrey identifies what was problematic about that basis of Thomas' connecting the Lord's Day to the fourth commandment and explores Reformation-era and seventeenth-century consideration of the Lord's Day, which better reflects the biblical witness concerning the holiness of a weekly Sabbath.

LEARNING GOALS

When you have finished this lesson, you should be able to:

- Identify what is flawed about Thomas Aquinas' basis for connecting the Lord's Day to the fourth commandment
- Understand how the Reformers reflected on the Lord's Day in reaction to the medieval church
- Summarize how the Lord's Day began to be understood in the late seventeenth century
- Describe the type of language that Scripture uses to convey the holiness of the weekly Sabbath

KEY IDEAS

- Thomas Aquinas connected the Lord's Day to the fourth commandment and established its continued observance on the basis of the church.
- The reflection of the Reformers concerning the Lord's Day and the fourth commandment must be understood in its historical context.
- By the seventeenth century, Reformed theologians had begun to see the Lord's Day as the Christian Sabbath.

- The holiness of the weekly Sabbath is immediately seen in how Scripture describes what it signified and the penalties if it was not observed.

REFLECTION & DISCUSSION QUESTIONS

Before the Video

What Do You Think?

Take a moment to answer the following questions. They will prepare you for the lecture.

- Who ought to determine the days on which we are to worship God?

- Why is the question about the relationship between the Lord's Day and the fourth commandment important?

Scripture Reading

Remember the Sabbath day, to keep it holy. Six days you shall labor, and do all your work, but the seventh day is a Sabbath to the LORD your God. On it you shall not do any work, you, or your son, or your daughter, your male servant, or your female servant, or your livestock, or the sojourner who is within your gates. For in six days the LORD made heaven and earth, the sea, and all that is in them, and rested on the seventh day. Therefore the LORD blessed the Sabbath day and made it holy.

—Exodus 20:8–11

- What reason is given for remembering the Sabbath day?

During the Video

Answer the following questions while you watch the video. They will guide you through the lecture.

Thomas Aquinas and the Reformers *0:00–7:38*

- What was flawed about Thomas Aquinas' foundation for asserting why the Lord's Day ought to be observed?

- What influenced the reflection of such Reformers as Martin Luther and John Calvin concerning the Lord's Day and the Sabbath?

The Seventeenth Century and Beyond 7:38–14:00

- What is similar yet different about how Reformed theologians thought about the Lord's Day compared to how Thomas Aquinas thought about it?

- What was a remarkable result of the late-seventeenth-century Reformed understanding of the Lord's Day?

Strong Biblical Language *14:00–24:08*

- What did the Sabbath signify for the people of Israel? What was the penalty for not observing it?

- What two questions need to be answered to help us understand the proper relationship between the Sabbath and the Lord's Day?

After the Video

Answer the following questions after you have finished the lecture. They will help you identify and summarize the major points.

- What are the five periods of the church's thought about the Lord's Day?

  If you are in a group, have the members discuss what makes the church fathers' and the Reformers' reflection on the significance of the Lord's Day similar in terms of historical context and, in the same manner, how the historical situation of the medieval church and the seventeenth century is similar.

- Why is it important to read Calvin's statements about the Lord's Day in their historical context?

  If you are in a group, have the members discuss what types of activities people have thought are permissible or impermissible on the Lord's Day. Ask: If someone approaches the Lord's Day differently than we do, how should we react?

- How did Dr. Godfrey communicate the idea that the Sabbath is a picture of the gospel?

If you are in a group, have the members read the challenging passage in Numbers 15:32–36. Ask: How can the gospel be seen in this passage?

PRAYER

Commit what you have learned from God's Word in this lesson to prayer.

- Praise God that He is worthy of all our lives and our worship.
- Confess any reluctance to soberly assess the strong language of Scripture concerning the weekly Sabbath.
- Thank God for rest as a reminder of the gospel truth that we don't have to work for our salvation.
- Ask God for help in understanding the Bible's authority over all matters of faith and practice.

REVIEW QUIZ

Use these multiple-choice questions to measure what you learned from this lesson.

1. What was flawed in Thomas Aquinas' thought concerning the Lord's Day?
   a. Its connecting of the Lord's Day to the fourth commandment
   b. Its basis on the authority of God's commandments
   c. Its foundation on the authority of the church
   d. Its legalistic enforcement of the Lord's Day

2. Calvin's statements that the Lord's Day is not a holy day demonstrate his low regard for the Lord's Day.
   a. True
   b. False

3. What term is used in the Westminster Confession of Faith to describe the weekly Sabbath?
   a. Dominicus
   b. Our Great Portion
   c. Christian Sabbath
   d. God's Holy Day

4. Which period of thought was less encumbered by the historical issues in its reflection on the Lord's Day?
   a. The period of the early church fathers
   b. The period of the Protestant Reformers
   c. The period of seventeenth-century Reformed orthodoxy
   d. Both b and c

5. Disagreements about the relationship between the Lord's Day and the fourth commandment should be a point of contention and division among Christians.
    a. True
    b. False

6. What phrase from Exodus 31 underscores the significance of the Sabbath?
    a. "Remember the Sabbath day, to keep it holy."
    b. "Therefore the LORD your God commanded you to keep the Sabbath day."
    c. "Whoever does any work on the Sabbath day shall be put to death."
    d. "God blessed the seventh day and made it holy."

Answer Key—Historical & Biblical Reflections

REFLECTION & DISCUSSION QUESTIONS

Before the Video

What Do You Think?

These are personal questions. The answers should be based on your own knowledge and experience.

Scripture Reading

- What reason is given for remembering the Sabbath day?

  The reason given for remembering the Sabbath is that the Lord ceased from His work of creation on the Sabbath day. By doing so, He blessed the Sabbath day and made it holy. So God provides us with His own example as one of the primary reasons to remember the Sabbath day by keeping it holy.

During the Video

Thomas Aquinas and the Reformers

- What was flawed about Thomas Aquinas' foundation for asserting why the Lord's Day ought to be observed?

  Thomas Aquinas, while using a valid distinction in the law to connect the Lord's Day to the Sabbath, thought that the Lord's Day was to be observed only because it was instituted by the church and was the customary practice of Christians.

- What influenced the reflection of such Reformers as Martin Luther and John Calvin concerning the Lord's Day and the Sabbath?

  Luther and Calvin were both influenced in the way they thought about the Lord's Day through extensive reading of the church fathers and their proximity to the medieval church. The church in that day believed it had the right to establish holy days, which is exactly what Thomas Aquinas thought had taken place with the establishment of the Lord's Day.

The Seventeenth Century and Beyond

- What is similar yet different about how Reformed theologians thought about the Lord's Day compared to how Thomas Aquinas thought about it?

  Reformed theologians, unlike Thomas, did not think that the Lord's Day was to be observed based on the authority of the church. Like Thomas, they did see a valid connection between the fourth commandment and the Lord's Day based on the ceremonial and moral distinction of the law, but unlike Thomas, they rooted the necessity of observing the Lord's Day as the Christian Sabbath in God's command. Also, the historical situation of the seventeenth century was somewhat similar to that of the medieval church; no perceived threat was influencing reflection on the connection between the Lord's Day and the fourth commandment.

- What was a remarkable result of the late-seventeenth-century Reformed understanding of the Lord's Day?

  Dr. Godfrey remarked that Reformed piety in observing the Lord's Day as a day set apart for rest unto worship created the best-educated laity in the history of the church. On the Lord's Day, people attended worship and had time to study, read, and learn the Bible and to perform other Christian works.

Strong Biblical Language

- What did the Sabbath signify for the people of Israel? What was the penalty for not observing it?

  The Sabbath signified the covenant that God had made with His people Israel and pointed to the reality that He was the One who sanctified them. The penalty for not observing the Sabbath—a day that would otherwise lead to refreshment—was death.

- What two questions need to be answered to help us understand the proper relationship between the Sabbath and the Lord's Day?

  The first question: Is the Sabbath in the Old Testament simply a Mosaic institution? The second question: What are we to make of those texts in the New Testament that seem to teach that all days are alike in the new covenant?

After the Video

- What are the five periods of the church's thought about the Lord's Day?

  The first period is reflected in the thought of the post-Apostolic church fathers, who did not connect the Lord's Day to the fourth commandment in part because of the historical moment and the necessity of distinguishing Christianity from Judaism. The second period is reflected in the thought of Thomas Aquinas in the medieval church, which did connect the Lord's Day to the fourth commandment, though it established Lord's Day observance on the basis of the church's authority. The third period is reflected in the thought of the Reformers during the Protestant Reformation, and like the church fathers, their statements about the Lord's Day have to be understood in their historical context. The fourth period is reflected in the thought of seventeenth-century Reformed confessions, which understood the Lord's Day to be the Christian Sabbath. The final period is reflected in the thought of our own day, which by and large doesn't understand the significance of the Lord's Day.

- Why is it important to read Calvin's statements about the Lord's Day in their historical context?

  Many people attempt to put Calvin at odds with Reformed thinkers in the seventeenth century when it comes to issues such as the Lord's Day. But if we read Calvin in light of his historical context, then his statements that the Lord's Day was not a holy day make sense. He was reacting against the Roman Catholic Church's assertion that the church has the right to determine holy days. When we read the breadth of Calvin's thought on the Lord's Day, we see that he considers it a day to be set apart for worship, which requires us to pause from everyday life, a position very close to that found in the Westminster Confession of Faith.

- How did Dr. Godfrey communicate the idea that the Sabbath is a picture of the gospel?

  After reading Exodus 31:12–17, Dr. Godfrey emphasized the language of the passage and its stress on God's own priority of the weekly Sabbath as a lesson that it is the Lord who sanctifies His people and gives them rest. Resting is intimately related to the gospel and how God works in our lives. We don't work to save ourselves. God does all the work.

REVIEW QUIZ

1. **C.**
   Many things were right about Thomas Aquinas' thought about the Lord's Day, primarily his connecting it to the fourth commandment and his distinction between the moral and ceremonial elements of that law. Yet, he rested the establishment of the Lord's Day not on the authority of God but on the authority of the church, which does not have the authority to declare holy days.

2. **B.**
   Calvin was reacting to the church's claim to authoritatively declare holy days. His statements must be understood within the context of the Reformation era and its struggle to promote the final authority of God's Word over church tradition. Calvin reverently understood the Lord's Day as a day to be set apart for worship.

3. **C.**
   The Westminster Confession of Faith calls the first day of the week the "Christian Sabbath." This term succinctly conveys the position on the Lord's Day found in the confession and its stress on the connection between the Lord's Day and the fourth commandment.

4. **C.**
   Like the early church fathers who were reacting to the delicate relationship between the church, Judaism, and the Mosaic law, the Reformers were reacting to their own historical context and the Roman Catholic Church's assertion that it had the authority to declare holy days. Like the medieval church, however, theologians in

the seventeenth century were further removed from historical conflicts in their reflection about the Lord's Day.

5. **B.**
   In this lesson, Dr. Godfrey prescribed charity as the appropriate posture when it comes to disagreements about the nature of the Lord's Day. This does not preclude open theological discussions with fellow Christians, but these should be undertaken with a charitable spirit.

6. **C.**
   All these passages underscore the importance of the Sabbath. Two of them are from the Ten Commandments in Exodus and Deuteronomy, respectively. Another is from Genesis 2 after God ceased creating. Many significant phrases in Exodus 31:12–17 showcase the importance of the Sabbath. It is a sign of God's covenant with His people and a reminder that He is the Lord who sanctifies them. Exodus 31 also prescribes the penalty of death for violating the Sabbath.

3

The Origin of the Sabbath

INTRODUCTION

Is the Sabbath simply a Mosaic institution? The biblical data suggests that the weekly Sabbath actually goes back further than Moses, all the way back to creation. In this lesson, Dr. Godfrey defends the position that the weekly Sabbath is a creation ordinance through an examination of key texts, discusses the implications of this truth, and introduces what appear to be New Testament difficulties for this position.

LEARNING GOALS

When you have finished this lesson, you should be able to:

- Understand the argument for the weekly Sabbath as a creation ordinance
- Identify the implications of the weekly Sabbath as a creation ordinance
- Interpret Romans 14:5–6, a passage in the New Testament that seems to teach that all days are alike in the new covenant, with respect to its context

KEY IDEAS

- God established the weekly Sabbath at creation as a pattern for us.
- The weekly Sabbath is a creation ordinance and not grounded solely in the Mosaic covenant.
- Romans 14:5–6, which appears to challenge the enduring nature of the weekly Sabbath, must be understood within the context of Paul's larger argument related to the weaker and stronger brother.

REFLECTION & DISCUSSION QUESTIONS

Before the Video

What Do You Think?

Take a moment to answer the following questions. They will prepare you for the lecture.

- As humans, how do we mark time? Where does the idea of a year, a month, or a day come from? What about the seven-day week?

- If the weekly Sabbath is rooted in creation, then what does that mean for all people?

Scripture Reading

Observe the Sabbath day, to keep it holy, as the LORD your God commanded you. Six days you shall labor and do all your work, but the seventh day is a Sabbath to the LORD your God. On it you shall not do any work, you or your son or your daughter or your male servant or your female servant, or your ox or your donkey or any of your livestock, or the sojourner who is within your gates, that your male servant and your female servant may rest as well as you. You shall remember that you were a slave in the land of Egypt, and the LORD your God brought you out from there with a mighty hand and an outstretched arm. Therefore the LORD your God commanded you to keep the Sabbath day.

—Deuteronomy 5:12–15

- What reason is given for observing the Sabbath day? How is this different from the fourth commandment in the book of Exodus?

During the Video

Answer the following questions while you watch the video. They will guide you through the lecture.

The Sabbath: A Mosaic Institution? *0:00–16:30*

- Why is it important to observe the difference between the reasons given for the fourth commandment in the books of Exodus and Deuteronomy?

- What is unique about the seven-day week compared to other ways that we mark time?

- What is significant about the relationship between Exodus 16 and 20?

Paul's Larger Argument *16:30–25:17*

- What is Paul's primary concern in Romans 14:5–6, based on its context?

- What type of "days" is Paul likely referring to in Romans 14:5–6?

After the Video

Answer the following questions after you have finished the lecture. They will help you identify and summarize the major points.

- How have some argued around the idea of the Sabbath commandment as a creation ordinance? How can our understanding of who God is and whom the weekly Sabbath is for provide an answer?

  If you are in a group, have the members read Mark 2:23–28. Ask: How does this passage explicitly underscore whom the weekly Sabbath is for? How should that inform the way we approach the weekly Sabbath? Also, how might this passage be used to clarify why the weekly Sabbath is now observed on the Lord's Day?

- How was the Sabbath at the beginning full of "eschatological expectation"?

  If you are in a group, have the members read Hebrews 3:7–4:10. Ask: What type of rest do you think the author of Hebrews has in mind?

- What is a common misunderstanding about the way we think about the Sabbath in the Old Testament? How might that inform the way you approach the Lord's Day today?

  If you are in a group, have the members discuss whether they think Paul's instruction about weaker and stronger brothers has practical application for how we relate to others who have varying beliefs about and practices on the Lord's Day.

PRAYER

Commit what you have learned from God's Word in this lesson to prayer.

- Praise God that He is eternally blessed and in need of nothing for His perfection.
- Confess any sinful reactions you might have had to the idea of the fourth commandment's lasting significance as based in creation.
- Thank God for providing you with a pattern to live your life that is intended to bless you.
- Ask God to help you see the Lord's Day as His gift to you.

REVIEW QUIZ

Use these multiple-choice questions to measure what you learned from this lesson.

1. Which passage does *not* connect the Sabbath to creation?
   a. The seventh-day rest in Genesis 2
   b. The fourth commandment in Exodus 20
   c. The fourth commandment in Deuteronomy 5
   d. The call to observe the Sabbath in Exodus 31

2. What is *not* true about the nature of the weekly Sabbath?
   a. It is a Mosaic institution.
   b. It is a creation ordinance.
   c. It is a pattern for our lives.
   d. It is a part of God's moral law.

3. The seven-day week cannot be explained in the same way as other ways of marking time can be.
   a. True
   b. False

4. What is Paul's primary concern in Romans 14:5–6?
   a. Feast days
   b. The weekly Sabbath
   c. Food and drink
   d. Worship

5. If we had never fallen in Adam, we would have still observed the Sabbath.
   a. True
   b. False

6. Which of the following New Testament passages most supports the view that the Sabbath is a creation ordinance?
   a. "As was his custom, [Jesus] went to the synagogue on the Sabbath day" (Luke 4:16).
   b. "The Sabbath was made for man, not man for the Sabbath" (Mark 2:27).
   c. "The Son of Man is lord even of the Sabbath" (Mark 2:28).
   d. "It is lawful to do good on the Sabbath" (Matt. 12:12).

Answer Key—The Origin of the Sabbath

REFLECTION & DISCUSSION QUESTIONS

Before the Video

What Do You Think?

These are personal questions. The answers should be based on your own knowledge and experience.

Scripture Reading

- What reason is given for observing the Sabbath day? How is this different from the fourth commandment in the book of Exodus?

  The reason given in this passage for observing the Sabbath day is God's redeeming Israel from captivity in Egypt. This passage highlights a redemptive reason for observing the Sabbath. In our previous Scripture reading of the fourth commandment in the book of Exodus, the reason given for the commandment is God's own model for us at creation.

During the Video

The Sabbath: A Mosaic Institution?

- Why is it important to observe the difference between the reasons given for the fourth commandment in the books of Exodus and Deuteronomy?

  The most foundational issue that determines our view of the Sabbath is how we think about its origin. Observing the difference between the reasons given for the fourth commandment is important because it brings the origin of the weekly Sabbath in view. Exodus roots the fourth commandment in God's creative work and rest. Deuteronomy, on the other hand, calls us to observe the Sabbath based on God's redemptive work. Both are important, but if Deuteronomy were taken alone, one might get the impression that the weekly Sabbath was only for Israel, a Mosaic institution.

- What is unique about the seven-day week compared to other ways that we mark time?

  The seven-day week as a pattern of our lives is established by God's special revelation. Other ways that we mark time are observed, generally, because of natural revelation. A year is one revolution of the earth around the sun. Our months are related to the moon's orbit. The twenty-four-hour day is determined by the earth's rotation on its axis. All these are established by nature, but the seven-day weekly pattern is established by God's special revelation.

- What is significant about the relationship between Exodus 16 and 20?

  The Ten Commandments are given in Exodus 20, which includes the formal codification of the Sabbath commandment. Exodus 16, however, indicates that Israel was observing the Sabbath before the giving of God's law at Sinai. This provides one more argument for why the weekly Sabbath is a creation ordinance.

Paul's Larger Argument

- What is Paul's primary concern in Romans 14:5–6, based on its context?

  Paul's primary concern is not with a weekly Sabbath. The context of this passage informs us that his primary concern is food and drink and the love that brothers and sisters in Christ ought to show one another concerning these things.

- What type of "days" is Paul likely referring to in Romans 14:5–6?

  Because this passage fits within Paul's larger argument concerning food and drink and the relationship between weaker and stronger Christians, the type of "days" that Paul has in mind is not the weekly Sabbath. If we understand these days to connect to the way that a weaker or stronger Christian relates to food and drink, then it is likely that Paul is referring to various days of fasting and prayer that were observed for the sake of Christian conscience.

After the Video

- How have some argued around the idea of the Sabbath commandment as a creation ordinance? How can our understanding of who God is and whom the weekly Sabbath is for provide an answer?

  Everyone has to acknowledge that the Sabbath is important in the opening chapters of the Bible. That God blessed the Sabbath day and made it holy does not convince everyone that the Sabbath commandment finds its origin in creation and is thus a creation ordinance. Someone might argue that the Sabbath day in Genesis 2 is not presented as a command and is presented that way only in the Mosaic law. A thoughtful response to this would reflect on who God is as God, who exists eternally blessed without a need for a day set apart as though it added anything to Him. God blessed the Sabbath day for us, and it therefore establishes the pattern of our lives.

- How was the Sabbath at the beginning full of "eschatological expectation"?

  Reformed theologians have understood that the Sabbath plants in our very being the idea that we are not done, that we are not finished, and this even before the fall. The Sabbath as a creation ordinance had an end point in mind. Even if sin had not entered into the world through Adam, the pattern of work and rest pointed forward to a greater perfection of rest than could ever be experienced from the initial creation.

- What is a common misunderstanding about the way we think about the Sabbath in the Old Testament? How might that inform the way you approach the Lord's Day today?

A common misunderstanding about the Sabbath in the Old Testament is that it was highly regulated with detailed rules for every aspect of what was permissible and not permissible on that day. The basic command of the Sabbath day was to not do any work. Understanding this may help you to think about the Lord's Day as more than a day of dos and don'ts.

REVIEW QUIZ

1. **C.**
   All these passages connect the Sabbath to God's creative work except the fourth commandment in Deuteronomy 5. In this second giving of the law, the reason provided for observing the fourth commandment is God's redeeming Israel from slavery in Egypt.

2. **A.**
   The purpose of tracing the fourth commandment back to God's creative work in the book of Genesis was to demonstrate how it is not a Mosaic institution. It was not merely a law for Israel. Israel observed the Sabbath before Sinai, and God established it as a pattern for our lives at creation. This provides significant weight to the argument that it has enduring significance as part of God's moral law.

3. **A.**
   We can explain why we mark time in years, months, and days. All these are products of natural revelation and based on astronomical cycles. The seven-day week, however, cannot be explained in these terms. It is something that God specially revealed at creation as the pattern for our lives.

4. **C.**
   Dr. Godfrey said that the special days that Paul references in Romans 14:5–6 are "almost incidental." They are not Paul's primary concern, and he is not talking about the Lord's Day. In the context of the passage, Paul is dealing with the relationship between a stronger and a weaker brother when it comes to matters of Christian conscience, primarily related to food and drink.

5. **A.**
   Because the one-in-seven-day rest is rooted in creation and is the pattern for our lives, it would have been observed by us even if we had not fallen in Adam. Even apart from sin, the Sabbath points forward to a fuller rest than could have ever been enjoyed in creation alone.

6. **B.**
   Dr. Godfrey alluded to Jesus' declaration in Mark 2:27 in this lesson when he was arguing for the Sabbath as a creation ordinance. In this declaration, Jesus says that the Sabbath was made for all people and not Israel alone.

4

Answers to Difficulties

INTRODUCTION

Many question the enduring nature of the fourth commandment because of passages in the New Testament. In Romans 14:5, for instance, Paul speaks permissibly about those who esteem "all days alike." Does he have the weekly Sabbath in mind here? What about when he refers to "days" in Galatians 4:10 or especially to "a Sabbath" in Colossians 2:16? In this lesson, Dr. Godfrey walks you through these passages to defend the continued relevance of a weekly Sabbath for the people of God.

LEARNING GOALS

When you have finished this lesson, you should be able to:

- Summarize answers to three difficult texts as they relate to the fourth commandment
- Explain the pattern of shadow and substance between the old and new covenants

KEY IDEAS

- The context of Romans 14:5–6 is key for interpreting what Paul means when he speaks permissibly of Christians' treating all days alike.
- The Galatians were susceptible to a teaching that insisted that the Mosaic law, including its various religious festivals, be kept in order for one to be justified.
- The seventh-day Sabbath is fulfilled in Sunday, as the creation ordinance shifts in the new covenant to the day of Christ's resurrection.

REFLECTION & DISCUSSION QUESTIONS

Before the Video

What Do You Think?

Take a moment to answer the following questions. They will prepare you for the lecture.

- What various holidays or special occasions do you observe that, while permissible, are not biblically required?

- What is the relationship between your justification and your obedience to the fourth commandment?

Scripture Reading

> *Now on the first day of the week Mary Magdalene came to the tomb early, while it was still dark, and saw that the stone had been taken away from the tomb. . . . But Mary stood weeping outside the tomb, and as she wept she stooped to look into the tomb. . . . Jesus said to her, "Woman, why are you weeping? Whom are you seeking?" Supposing him to be the gardener, she said to him, "Sir, if you have carried him away, tell me where you have laid him, and I will take him away." Jesus said to her, "Mary." She turned and said to him in Aramaic, "Rabboni!" (which means Teacher). . . . On the evening of that day, the first day of the week, the doors being locked where the disciples were for fear of the Jews, Jesus came and stood among them and said to them, "Peace be with you." . . . Eight days later, his disciples were inside again, and Thomas was with them. Although the doors were locked, Jesus came and stood among them and said, "Peace be with you." Then he said to Thomas, "Put your finger here, and see my hands; and put out your hand, and place it in my side. Do not disbelieve, but believe." Thomas answered him, "My Lord and my God!"*
>
> —John 20:1, 11, 15–16, 19, 26–28

- What do these appearances of the resurrected Lord have in common?

During the Video

Answer the following questions while you watch the video. They will guide you through the lecture.

Paul's Larger Argument Continued *0:00–6:47*

- Why can it not be the case that Paul is referring to Jewish institutions in Romans 14:5–6?

"Days and Months and Seasons and Years" *6:47–11:57*

- What does Paul mean when he asks the Galatians, "Do you not listen to the law?" (Gal. 4:21)?

- What were the Galatians attempting to do by observing particular Mosaic days?

What about Colossians 2:16? *11:57–24:03*

- Why is Colossians 2:16 the most difficult text that seems to speak against the continued relevance of the fourth commandment?
- How does Dr. Godfrey interpret what Paul means in light of this difficulty?

After the Video

Answer the following questions after you have finished the lecture. They will help you identify and summarize the major points.

- How would you respond to someone who said that Paul's consternation that the Galatians "observe days and months and seasons and years" (4:10) means that all days should be treated alike?

  If you are in a group, have the members answer the following question: How does the tendency of the Galatian church help us rightly approach the Lord's Day?
- What is different about the rhythm of the believer's life in the new covenant as opposed to life in the old covenant?

  If you are in a group, have the members talk about how they can practically apply this truth in the way that they prepare for and enjoy the Lord's Day. Ask: How should this affect what we think, say, and do on the Lord's Day?
- Why are the categories of shadow and substance helpful for working through Paul's statement in Colossians 2:16?

  If you are in a group, have the members discuss the degree to which they are convinced that the Sabbath principle underwent a change from the seventh to the first day of the week.

PRAYER

Commit what you have learned from God's Word in this lesson to prayer.

- Praise God for His Word, which guides you into the truth.

- Confess any tendency you have to strive for a righteousness apart from Christ.
- Thank God for Christ's finished work, which you rest in each Lord's Day.
- Ask God to help you approach difficult texts of Scripture with humility and reliance on the Spirit's work to illumine them.

REVIEW QUIZ

Use these multiple-choice questions to measure what you learned from this lesson.

1. What is Paul's focus in Galatians 4:10?
   a. The weekly Sabbath
   b. The Mosaic calendar
   c. Weaker and stronger brothers
   d. The change from Sabbath to Lord's Day

2. If all days are alike in the new covenant, the fourth commandment no longer has any relevance.
   a. True
   b. False

3. How can we also fall into the Galatian problem with respect to the Lord's Day?
   a. By resting in Christ on the Lord's Day
   b. By refraining from work on the Lord's Day
   c. By keeping the Lord's Day self-righteously
   d. By worshiping on the Lord's Day

4. Which person purportedly had a vision that made Saturday worship a primary distinctive of Seventh-day Adventists?
   a. Joseph Smith
   b. Mary Baker Eddy
   c. Charles Taze Russell
   d. Ellen G. White

5. Colossians 2:16 is the most difficult passage concerning the nature of the Sabbath because it uses the word for "Sabbath."
   a. True
   b. False

6. What categories are introduced in Colossians 2:16–17 that help us to think about the relationship of the Sabbath to the Lord's Day?
   a. Already and not yet
   b. New covenant and old covenant
   c. Shadow and substance
   d. Physical and spiritual

Answer Key—Answers to Difficulties

REFLECTION & DISCUSSION QUESTIONS

Before the Video

What Do You Think?

These are personal questions. The answers should be based on your own knowledge and experience.

Scripture Reading

- What do these appearances of the resurrected Lord have in common?

  These appearances have many things in common. Each of them features a miraculous appearance of our Lord. Only upon hearing her name does Mary recognize Jesus, and He appeared among His disciples two times through locked doors. Twice, Jesus pronounces a blessing when appearing to His disciples, and twice, His followers make a profession about who He is (Mary and Thomas). Most importantly, as pertains to the Lord's Day, these appearances occur on the first day of the week. ("Eight days later" denotes a week. When Sunday, the "first" day, begins the sequence, the following Sunday is eight days later.)

During the Video

Paul's Larger Argument Continued

- Why can it not be the case that Paul is referring to Jewish institutions in Romans 14:5–6?

  In Romans 14:5–6, Paul has in mind special days that someone might set apart to abstain from certain foods and drink. No Jewish institutions call God's people to abstain from wine in observance of a particular day. Neither are there days on which people are called to eat only vegetables, which Paul is dealing with in the larger context of the passage (see Rom. 14:2).

"Days and Months and Seasons and Years"

- What does Paul mean when he asks the Galatians, "Do you not listen to the law?" (Gal. 4:21)?

  In Galatians, Paul deals with the improper use of the law. In doing this, he teaches us one of the reasons the law was given: "because of transgressions" (3:19). One of the functions of the law was to expose sin, so when Paul asks this question of the Galatians, he is trying to show them that the law declares them to be sinners.

- What were the Galatians attempting to do by observing particular Mosaic days?

  The Galatians were keeping various aspects of the Mosaic law to be justified through their obedience. They were trying to make themselves right with God while missing the point that the law actually works to condemn them.

What about Colossians 2:16?

- Why is Colossians 2:16 the most difficult text that seems to speak against the continued relevance of the fourth commandment?

  Colossians 2:16 is a formidable text because, unlike the others explored in this lesson, it uses the word "Sabbath." Though the term used for "Sabbath" is plural, only a few places in the New Testament use this plural term to refer to the seventh-day Sabbath.

- How does Dr. Godfrey interpret what Paul means in light of this difficulty?

  Instead of explaining away what the word for "Sabbath" could mean besides the seventh-day Sabbath, Dr. Godfrey confronts the challenge of Colossians 2:16 head on. He grants that it is referring to the seventh-day Sabbath, but he understands that day as fulfilled in Christ, while the first day of the week remains connected to the fourth commandment.

After the Video

- How would you respond to someone who said that Paul's consternation that the Galatians "observe days and months and seasons and years" (4:10) means that all days should be treated alike?

  Dr. Godfrey approached this text by building out the context of Paul's letters to the Galatians, showing that their primary issue was attempting to be justified by observing the Mosaic law. Paul is not referring to the weekly Sabbath, which is a creation ordinance; he is referring to other ceremonial days that have been fulfilled in Christ.

- What is different about the rhythm of the believer's life in the new covenant as opposed to life in the old covenant?

  In the old covenant, God's people rested on the seventh day after having worked six days. The pattern of their lives anticipated the rest of the seventh day of the week. In the new covenant, God's people rest and worship on the first day of the week because of the fulfillment that has already begun in Jesus Christ.

- Why are the categories of shadow and substance helpful for working through Paul's statement in Colossians 2:16?

  Throughout the Old Testament, certain things anticipated new covenant realities. They were shadows of the substance that would come in the new covenant. Circumcision is a shadow of baptism, and Israel is a shadow of the church, for instance. In the same way, the seventh-day Sabbath was a shadow of the rest we have in Christ, which is its substance. Christ has fulfilled it, shifting the Sabbath principle as a creation ordinance to the first day of the week, the day of His resurrection. Because it has been fulfilled, we already enjoy rest in Jesus Christ yet await its fullness in heaven and in the new heavens and new earth.

REVIEW QUIZ

1. **B.**
   In Galatians 4:10, Paul says, "You observe days and months and seasons and years!" This statement isn't about the Sabbath day; it is set within Paul's larger argument about the Galatians' striving to be justified by the law. The days, months, seasons, and years that Paul is talking about refer to the Mosaic calendar, which would have been considered necessary to keep to somehow attain a righteousness by the law.

2. **A.**
   This is at the heart of the argument against the enduring nature of the fourth commandment. If it could be demonstrated that the writers of the New Testament treated all days alike, then the relevance of the fourth commandment would disappear. The question is whether this claim holds up.

3. **C.**
   Worship and resting, both from work and in Christ, are right and appropriate on the Lord's Day. We would be like the Galatians, however, if we did those things to achieve a righteousness in ourselves. If that is our posture toward the Lord's Day, then we are not truly resting in Christ and His righteousness alone.

4. **D.**
   Dr. Godfrey noted that Seventh-day Adventists worship on Saturday because their prophetess, Ellen G. White, supposedly had a vision of the fourth commandment with a halo around it and concluded that the church had been disobedient for worshiping on Sunday.

5. **A.**
   Neither Romans 14:5–6 nor Galatians 4:10 uses the word for "Sabbath," and the context of these passages suggests that Paul does not have the weekly Sabbath in mind. Colossians 2:16, however, does use the word for "Sabbath," and though this word is plural, it refers to the seventh-day Sabbath.

6. **C.**
   Colossians 2:16–17 says, "Therefore let no one pass judgment on you in questions of food and drink, or with regard to a festival or a new moon or a Sabbath. These are a shadow of the things to come, but the substance belongs to Christ." Although this verse speaks of the seventh-day Sabbath as a shadow that had been fulfilled by its substance, which is Christ, it does not need to mean that the Sabbath principle as a creation ordinance has been done away with. It is now observed in the Lord's Day.

5

The Lord's Day as Sabbath

INTRODUCTION

The Sabbath on the seventh day has been fulfilled in the new covenant, yet the Lord's Day has been set apart for continued observance of the Sabbath principle found in creation. The Lord's Day is the first day of the week, and it is the day on which Christians have historically gathered—stretching all the way back to the Apostles—to worship the resurrected Christ. In this lesson, Dr. Godfrey examines the positive evidence of the New Testament that the Lord's Day is indeed special and of enduring relevance for Christians.

LEARNING GOALS

When you have finished this lesson, you should be able to:

- Demonstrate the uniqueness of the first day of the week from the New Testament
- Interpret what the author of Hebrews means by the following statement: "So then, there remains a Sabbath rest for the people of God" (4:9)
- Provide rationale for why the fourth commandment isn't explicitly mentioned in the New Testament

KEY IDEAS

- The New Testament's positive case for the connection between the Lord's Day and the fourth commandment must be understood cumulatively, taking all the data into consideration.
- The New Testament teaches that the "Lord's day," as named in Revelation 1:10, is the first day of the week when Christians gathered for worship.
- Our call to worship on the Lord's Day is not a matter of tradition but one of Apostolic practice.
- God has given us the Lord's Day as a blessing, that we might set aside the cares of this world and worship Him with His people.

REFLECTION & DISCUSSION QUESTIONS

Before the Video

What Do You Think?

Take a moment to answer the following questions. They will prepare you for the lecture.

- Considering Dr. Godfrey's previous treatment of challenging texts, are you convinced that the New Testament does not teach that all days are alike?
- How is the Lord's Day a blessing to you?

Scripture Reading

Oh come, let us worship and bow down; let us kneel before the Lord, our Maker! For he is our God, and we are the people of his pasture, and the sheep of his hand. Today, if you hear his voice, do not harden your hearts, as at Meribah, as on the day at Massah in the wilderness, when your fathers put me to the test and put me to the proof, though they had seen my work. For forty years I loathed that generation and said, "They are a people who go astray in their heart, and they have not known my ways." Therefore I swore in my wrath, "They shall not enter my rest."

—Psalm 95:6–11

- What is the "rest" referred to in this passage?

During the Video

Answer the following questions while you watch the video. They will guide you through the lecture.

A Special Day *0:00–9:03*

- What does Dr. Godfrey take John's being "in the Spirit" on the Lord's Day (Rev. 1:10) to mean?
- What does the grammar of the phrase "Lord's day" reveal about the significance of the day?
- What passages can be used to connect the Lord's Day and the first day of the week?

The Fulfilled yet Enduring Nature of the Sabbath *9:03–23:51*

- What does the author of Hebrews mean by a "Sabbath rest" that remains for the people of God?

- Why does the New Testament explicitly emphasize the second table of the law as opposed to the first?

- How should we understand Jesus' actions and statements about the Sabbath?

After the Video

Answer the following questions after you have finished the lecture. They will help you identify and summarize the major points.

- How does the simple phrase "Lord's day" undermine the idea that the New Testament writers taught that every day is alike in the new covenant? Why ought we to observe the Lord's Day?

  If you are in a group, have the members reflect on how the simple phrase "Lord's day" may help them rightly prioritize the things they do on Sundays.

- What are the implications of the meaning of "Sabbath rest" in Hebrews 4:9 and our understanding of the fourth commandment in the new covenant?

  If you are in a group, have the members read Revelation 4–5 and make observations about the heavenly worship that John witnessed in these chapters, the "Sabbath rest" of Hebrews, and how we ought to spend our weekly Lord's Day.

- How does Jesus' earthly ministry inform us of what God intended the Sabbath to be? Why is it important to remember this truth even today?

  If you are in a group, ask the members the following questions: What would be strange if Jesus were rejecting the Sabbath in His exchanges with the Pharisees? If He were doing this, would there be any negative implications for our doctrine of God, Christology, or soteriology?

PRAYER

Commit what you have learned from God's Word in this lesson to prayer.

- Praise God for His goodness as seen in His offer of a final Sabbath rest.
- Confess ways in which you have been legalistic about the Lord's Day.
- Thank God for giving the Lord's Day to you as a life-giving blessing.
- Ask God to give you opportunities to do acts of mercy on the Lord's Day.

REVIEW QUIZ

Use these multiple-choice questions to measure what you learned from this lesson.

1. The first day of the week has significance in the New Testament for all except which of the following?
   a. The resurrection of Jesus Christ
   b. The collection of alms for the poor
   c. The gathering of Christians to worship
   d. The early evangelism of Jews in synagogues
2. The "Lord's day" in Revelation 1:10 means the great eschatological "day of the Lord."
   a. True
   b. False
3. Which psalm is quoted by the author of Hebrews in Hebrews 4 when referring to "rest"?
   a. Psalm 119
   b. Psalm 110
   c. Psalm 95
   d. Psalm 73
4. Which theologian believed that Hebrews 4:9 alone established a weekly Sabbath in the new covenant?
   a. John Calvin
   b. Abraham Kuyper
   c. Martin Luther
   d. John Owen
5. Jesus criticized the legalism associated with the Sabbath and not the Sabbath itself.
   a. True
   b. False

6. Which is an example of the type of commandment explicitly reiterated in the New Testament?
    a. "You shall have no other gods before me" (Ex. 20:3).
    b. "You shall not take the name of the LORD your God in vain" (Ex. 20:7).
    c. "Remember the Sabbath day, to keep it holy" (Ex. 20:8).
    d. "Honor your father and your mother" (Ex. 20:12).

Answer Key—The Lord's Day as Sabbath

REFLECTION & DISCUSSION QUESTIONS

Before the Video

What Do You Think?

These are personal questions. The answers should be based on your own knowledge and experience.

Scripture Reading

- What is the "rest" referred to in this passage?

  Some key places ("Meribah" and "Massah in the wilderness") and phrases ("forty years" and "generation") indicate that Psalm 95 is referring to the wilderness generation of Israel who grumbled against the Lord and were not permitted to enter the Promised Land. "Rest," then, refers to the land in this context. Later in this lesson, Dr. Godfrey will discuss how the author of Hebrews speaks of "rest" in terms of a place.

During the Video

A Special Day

- What does Dr. Godfrey take John's being "in the Spirit" on the Lord's Day (Rev. 1:10) to mean?

  The phrase "in the Spirit," when understood in light of Revelation 4:2, means "worshiping." The whole of Revelation 4 is a great worship scene before the throne of God, so John was worshiping on the Lord's Day when he received his initial vision.

- What does the grammar of the phrase "Lord's day" reveal about the significance of the day?

  In the Greek phrase for "Lord's day," the word for "Lord" is actually the adjective kyriakos. *This adjective is used in only one other phrase: the "Lord's supper" (1 Cor. 11:20). Just as the Lord's Supper is an especially important meal, so must the Lord's Day be an especially important day.*

- What passages can be used to connect the Lord's Day and the first day of the week?

  No place in the New Testament calls the Lord's Day the first day of the week, but it is clear that this is when the Christians gathered, on the day on which our Lord rose again. Jesus' resurrection appearances on the first day are found in Matthew 28:1; Mark 16:2; Luke 24:1; and John 20:1, 19, 26. Christians therefore gathered to worship on the first day of the week (Acts 20:7; 1 Cor. 16:2), making the first day the most fitting day of the week to call the "Lord's day."

The Fulfilled yet Enduring Nature of the Sabbath

- What does the author of Hebrews mean by a "Sabbath rest" that remains for the people of God?

  In Psalm 95, the idea of rest is used to refer to the promised land, so the author of Hebrews in quoting this psalm, also has in mind a place or location. The "Sabbath rest" that the author of Hebrews has in mind for the people of God is heaven, the eternal rest of glory.

- Why does the New Testament explicitly emphasize the second table of the law as opposed to the first?

  In various places in the New Testament, the second table of the law (the fifth through tenth commandments) is reiterated, but commandments such as the fourth are not ever mentioned. One explanation for this is that perhaps that the new covenant people had more trouble with the matters pertaining to the second table of the law, or the matters of the first table of the law were implicitly understood and assumed naturally as part of their identity.

- How should we understand Jesus' actions and statements about the Sabbath?

  In the Gospels, it isn't uncommon to find Jesus doing things on the Sabbath that shocked the Pharisees. Jesus rejected pharisaical attitudes about the Sabbath, but He did not reject the Sabbath itself. Jesus was calling His people to understand the purpose of the Sabbath once again and see it as a delight and not a burden (see Isa. 58).

After the Video

- How does the simple phrase "Lord's day" undermine the idea that the New Testament writers taught that every day is alike in the new covenant? Why ought we to observe the Lord's Day?

  The phrase "Lord's day" by itself undermines the notion that all days are alike in the new covenant because it marks out one day of the week as special or belonging to the Lord. The phrase itself does not explicitly connect that day to the fourth commandment, but from the cumulative witness of the New Testament, we observe that the early church gathered to worship on Sundays from the time of the Apostles. The church today does not worship on Sundays as a mere custom but follows the Apostolic practice.

- What are the implications of the meaning of "Sabbath rest" in Hebrews 4:9 and our understanding of the fourth commandment in the new covenant?

  The phrase "Sabbath rest" in Hebrews 4:9 refers to the ultimate, heavenly eschatological rest that we will enjoy in the intermediate state and embodied in the new heavens and new earth. It is significant that we are called to look forward to this reality, which is described as "Sabbath." The concept of the Sabbath is therefore not irrelevant to the new covenant. Just as the Sabbath is foundational to creation, it is also the fulfillment of all that God is doing in history. It makes sense, then, that the Lord's Day would be observed as a continuation of the moral aspects of the fourth commandment.

- How does Jesus' earthly ministry inform us of what God intended the Sabbath to be? Why is it important to remember this truth even today?

  During His earthly ministry, Jesus often confronted the Pharisees' Sabbath legalism by healing on the Sabbath. Jesus was not, however, doing away with the Sabbath through these acts but demonstrating what the Sabbath was for. It was not about an endless list of dos and don'ts; it was to be a delight for people, a day of rest and replenishment. This emphasis of Jesus' ministry must still be kept in mind today to protect us from a mindset of legalism, wherein we treat the Lord's Day as something we keep for the sake of attaining our own righteousness.

REVIEW QUIZ

1. **D.**
   When the Apostle Paul entered a new town on his missionary journeys, he would first visit the local synagogues to preach the gospel among the Jews before going out to the gentiles. Such a gathering would not have occurred on the first day of the week.

2. **B.**
   Revelation 1:10 says that John was "in the Spirit on the Lord's day." The grammar behind the phrase "Lord's day" is not the same as for what could be otherwise translated "day of the Lord" to refer to the day of the Lord's return and the judgment and consummation of all things. "Lord's day" refers instead to the first day of the week, when Christians gathered to worship in celebration of the resurrection.

3. **C.**
   The author of Hebrews frequently quotes from the book of Psalms, quoting from it six times in the first chapter alone. In Hebrews 4, he quotes from Psalm 95, which references Israel's disobedience in the wilderness. Canaan, the land that the wilderness generation was not permitted to enter, is understood to be the "rest" in this psalm.

4. **D.**
   Dr. Godfrey pointed to John Owen's multivolume commentary on the book of Hebrews as setting forth an argument that Hebrews 4:9 ("There remains a Sabbath rest for the people of God") is enough to establish the weekly Sabbath. Dr. Godfrey used Hebrews 4:9 as support for the continued relevance of the fourth commandment, but he understands Hebrews 4:9 to be referring to an ultimate, heavenly spiritual rest.

5. **A.**
The Pharisees often set traps for our Lord to see whether He would heal on the Sabbath, and thus violate it in their minds. These Pharisees failed to understand the Sabbath, and Jesus' works, far from undermining the fourth commandment, underscored its true purpose.

6. **D.**
A correct answer to this question requires an inference in identifying which commandments belong to the second table of the law (the fifth through the tenth commandments). In this lesson, Dr. Godfrey brought up the common objection that the New Testament writers explicitly reiterate the second table of the law but not the first, thus weakening the case that the fourth commandment has any enduring significance.

6

Living It Out

INTRODUCTION

Just as with the Sabbath, the Lord's Day should not be thought of as a list of dos and don'ts. Yet there is an element of duty when it comes to the Lord's Day, and Reformed confessional and catechetical statements about the Lord's Day and the fourth commandment help orient us to its purpose. In this lesson, Dr. Godfrey surveys Reformed confessions and catechisms, as well as Psalm 92, to teach us how any duty on the Lord's Day ought to translate to delight.

LEARNING GOALS

When you have finished this lesson, you should be able to:

- Summarize the general teaching of Reformed confessions and catechisms about the Lord's Day
- Apply the teaching of the Reformed confessional material practically to your life
- Explain what Psalm 92 calls us to in our Sabbath rest and worship

KEY IDEAS

- The Heidelberg Catechism, the Canons of Dort, and the Westminster Confession of Faith each emphasize our obligation to worship on the Lord's Day.
- Psalm 92 informs us how we ought to enjoy our Lord's Day by focusing on God and His wondrous works, even on His judgment.
- God has given us the Lord's Day to renew and rejuvenate us from all the wasted time of the world.

REFLECTION & DISCUSSION QUESTIONS

Before the Video

What Do You Think?

Take a moment to answer the following questions. They will prepare you for the lecture.

- How do you prepare for the Lord's Day?

- What has been the most interesting thing you have learned thus far in your study of the Sabbath and Lord's Day?

Scripture Reading

If you turn back your foot from the Sabbath, from doing your pleasure on my holy day, and call the Sabbath a delight and the holy day of the Lord honorable; if you honor it, not going your own ways, or seeking your own pleasure, or talking idly; then you shall take delight in the Lord, and I will make you ride on the heights of the earth; I will feed you with the heritage of Jacob your father, for the mouth of the Lord has spoken.

—Isaiah 58:13–14

- What is at the heart of true observance of the Sabbath in this passage?

During the Video

Answer the following questions while you watch the video. They will guide you through the lecture.

Reformed Standards *0:00–9:35*

- What ultimate rest does the Heidelberg Catechism point us to enjoy throughout our lives?

- What types of works do the Canons of Dort call us to rest from on the Lord's Day?

- Which Reformed confession or catechism seems to be the strictest in what it calls us to observe on the Lord's Day? How so?

Psalm 92: A Song for the Sabbath *9:35–24:02*

- What call to us does Psalm 92 open with after its thanksgiving?
- How can pondering judgment and wickedness possibly be good for our Lord's Day?

After the Video

Answer the following questions after you have finished the lecture. They will help you identify and summarize the major points.

- What most stood out to you from the various statements read from the Reformed confessions and catechism concerning the Lord's Day? Why?

  If you are in a group, have the members discuss the types of things they usually talk about with one another before or after worship. Ask: What would be some of the benefits of talking more directly about the worship service or the sermon with one another? Could there be any possible drawbacks?
- Why do you think Psalm 92 mentions wickedness in connection to the Sabbath?

  If you are in a group, have the members read Psalm 73. Ask: Though the psalmist initially "almost stumbled," what are some of the benefits that he reaped from his experience? Have you ever experienced something like this?
- How is duty on the Lord's Day not a bad thing, yet not everything?

  If you are in a group, have each member identify the most important concept he or she has learned in this teaching series, and discuss the significance of these concepts.

PRAYER

Commit what you have learned from God's Word in this lesson to prayer.

- Praise God for His care for us as His people, remembering the work He has done.
- Confess ways that you have thought about the duty of the Lord's Day begrudgingly.
- Thank God that His care is reflected to you in the blessings of an entire day to free you from the world.
- Ask God to help you find ways to set apart the Lord's Day as holy, whether it be in how you prepare for it or in how you live on it.

REVIEW QUIZ

Use these multiple-choice questions to measure what you learned from this lesson.

1. Which Reformed confession or catechism utilizes Thomas Aquinas' ceremonial/moral distinction for describing the fourth commandment?
   a. Heidelberg Catechism
   b. Canons of Dort
   c. Westminster Confession of Faith
   d. Westminster Larger Catechism

2. Which Reformed confession or catechism calls for an ordering of affairs before the Lord's Day?
   a. Heidelberg Catechism
   b. Canons of Dort
   c. Westminster Confession of Faith
   d. Westminster Shorter Catechism

3. It is legalistic to talk about the duty Christians have to God on the Lord's Day.
   a. True
   b. False

4. Which Reformed confession or catechism emphasizes a resting from "evil works" in connection to the fourth commandment?
   a. Heidelberg Catechism
   b. Canons of Dort
   c. Westminster Confession of Faith
   d. Westminster Shorter Catechism

5. The title of Psalm 92 is the only place the Sabbath is mentioned in the entire book of Psalms.
   a. True
   b. False

6. In what book of the Psalter is Psalm 92 located?
   a. Book 2
   b. Book 3
   c. Book 4
   d. Book 5

Answer Key—Living It Out

REFLECTION & DISCUSSION QUESTIONS

Before the Video

What Do You Think?

These are personal questions. The answers should be based on your own knowledge and experience.

Scripture Reading

- What is at the heart of true observance of the Sabbath in this passage?

  In this passage, the Lord upholds the Sabbath day as holy before His people, and twice the word "delight" is used, both for a delight in the Sabbath and for a delight in the Lord as the result of delight in the Sabbath.

During the Video

Reformed Standards

- What ultimate rest does the Heidelberg Catechism point us to enjoy throughout our lives?

  The Heidelberg Catechism, while calling us to observe specific things on the Lord's Day in obedience to the fourth commandment, also points us to a rest that ought to characterize our entire Christian lives. We are to rest from our evil works and allow the Holy Spirit to work in our lives in anticipation of the eternal Sabbath.

- What types of works do the Canons of Dort call us to rest from on the Lord's Day?

  The Canons of Dort use the language of "servile works," which means "all ordinary labors," in calling us to set apart the Lord's Day as holy. Positively, the Canons of Dort call us to worship and to works of mercy and necessity.

- Which Reformed confession or catechism seems to be the strictest in what it calls us to observe on the Lord's Day? How so?

  The Canons of Dort and the Westminster Confession of Faith share much in common in their statements about the Lord's Day. The Westminster Confession, however, calls us to use the whole day for worship.

Psalm 92: A Song for the Sabbath

- What call to us does Psalm 92 open with after its thanksgiving?

  Psalm 92, after the thanksgiving of the psalmist, opens with a challenge for us to remember the Lord, to focus our thoughts and lives on Him and His wondrous works: "It is good to give thanks to the Lord, *to sing praises to your name, O Most High; to declare your steadfast love in the morning, and your faithfulness by night. . . . For you, O* Lord, *have made me glad by your work; at the works of your hands I sing for joy. How great are your works, O* Lord! *Your thoughts are very deep!" (vv. 1–2, 4–5).*

- How can pondering judgment and wickedness possibly be good for our Lord's Day?

  Just as Psalm 92 calls us to remember the works of the Lord, it also calls us to reflect on God's righteous judgment of the wicked: "For behold, your enemies, O Lord, *for behold, your enemies shall perish; all evildoers shall be scattered" (v. 9). This is a good reminder to us that the wickedness of the world will come to an end and that we will have true rest on account of this. Such reflection may also lead us to have greater zeal for evangelizing the lost.*

After the Video

- What most stood out to you from the various statements read from the Reformed confessions and catechism concerning the Lord's Day? Why?

  The answer to this question is personal, but it should include reference to the Heidelberg Catechism, the Canons of Dort, or the Westminster Confession of Faith.

- Why do you think Psalm 92 mentions wickedness in connection to the Sabbath?

  Psalm 92 is about the Sabbath, and it reflects on God's righteous judgment of the wicked. Dr. Godfrey elaborated that reflecting on this judgment ourselves is a helpful reminder that God is in control and that wickedness will not long flourish. Even in history, God has displayed that judgment temporally. A deep connection between God's judgment of the wicked and the Sabbath may be found in the idea of the Sabbath as rest. We will have a fullness of rest when God judges both His and our own enemies.

- How is duty on the Lord's Day not a bad thing, yet not everything?

  There are elements of duty when it comes to the Lord's Day. We observe the Lord's Day in keeping with the fourth commandment. God calls us to this. Even when we do not feel worshipful on the Lord's Day, we are still called to worship God. Fulfilling our duty in this regard can lead to great blessing, if worship changes the way we feel positively, for example. Yet such duty is not everything and is never enough when it comes to our worship of God and our obedience to His commands. He calls us to be obedient from the heart, and He calls us to delight in the Lord's Day.

REVIEW QUIZ

1. **B.**
   Though the distinction between ceremonial and moral aspects of the law is at work in each of these statements, the Canons of Dort explicitly appeal to this distinction to explain how it is that the fourth commandment may be observed on the first day of the week.

2. **C.**
   The Westminster Standards, which include the confession and larger and shorter catechisms, prioritize our need to keep the Lord's Day, as the Christian Sabbath, holy. One of the things that the Westminster Confession of Faith prescribes to help us do this is the ordering of our "common affairs" the day before.

3. **B.**
   Duty comes with all God's commands, so considering the duty we have as Christians on the Lord's Day is not purely legalistic. God calls us to rest and worship on the Lord's Day. That being said, God does not call us to a heartless observance of that day. Our duty ought to be coupled with delight.

4. **A.**
   The idea that we must turn from our sin and strive for obedience is certainly affirmed in each of these statements. The Heidelberg Catechism, however, uses this phrase in connection with how we ought to live out the fourth commandment, which requires that "all the days of my life I rest from my evil works, let the Lord work in me by His Holy Spirit, and thus begin, in this life, the eternal Sabbath."

5. **A.**
   As hard as it may be to believe, the title of Psalm 92 is the only place the Sabbath is mentioned in the book of Psalms. Dr. Godfrey drew out an implication from the Sabbath's being mentioned only in the psalm's title: The Sabbath is a call to reflect endlessly not on the Sabbath but on God Himself.

6. **C.**
   Dr. Godfrey's book Learning to Love the Psalms *is a helpful resource that orients us to the structure of the book of Psalms. The book of Psalms is divided into five books, each of which has its own particular emphases. Psalm 92 is located in Book 4, which reflects on the difficult times that the people of God can live in, yet this psalm is marked by calmness.*